Five Steps to Birthing
Your Dream
A Spiritual Midwife's Manual

Written by:
Christine Gilliam Hornback

To: Connie

From: Natalie

You have greatness
with in you!

5 Steps to Birthing Your Dream A Spiritual Midwife's Manual
by Christine Gilliam Hornback
Copyright©2016 by Christine Gilliam Hornback
http://www.covenantessentials.com
All rights reserved
Published in the United States of America
No part of this publication may be reproduced, stored in a retrieval system or transmitted in any way by any means, electronic, mechanical, photo copy, recording or otherwise without prior permission of the author except as provided by USA Copyright Law

All Scripture References taken from the King James Version of The Holy Bible.

Dedications

I dedicate this book to all of the Dreamers! My desire is to Inspire One Dreamer at a Time! I dedicate this book to those of you who have seen your dreams come true and for those who may be weary in waiting. May this book help encourage you to dream a new dream or to see a fulfillment of your lifelong dreams!

⍰

Endorsements

Atlanta Revival Center

Chris Hornback (Christine) is a woman of faith and prayer. She loves Jesus with a passion that is contagious and infectious. I have personally known Chris for 17 years and been her pastor. She has raised two amazing sons with her husband Richard. God promised her children. Chris and Richard had children after being married for 20 years. After having Caleb her first son, she was so blessed but knew that she was promised another child. She went through many disappointments and it looked as if she should be content with her awesome son Caleb. She determined in her heart it was time to push. This BOOK is about not accepting part of the promise but going all the way until you have everything God has for your life. I highly recommend reading this book to encourage you in your walk of faith. **~Pastor Vance Murphy**
http://www.atlantarevivalcenter.com/

Lakeview Times Online Weekly Newspaper & Magazine
Christine has been a weekly or regular contributor to Lakeview Times for the past few years. 5 Steps to Birthing a Dream A Spiritual Midwife's Manual is a further outreach of the kind of articles she writes. It was an amazingly easy to read book written for women but men will love it too." **~Greg Hetherington, Lakeviewtimes.com**
http://www.lakeviewtimes.com
http://www.loldirectory.com/

J.C. Beaver, Author

"I was in need of the 5 Steps to Birthing Your Dream A Spiritual Midwife's Manual, when I received my copy. I read it, and then I re-read it with my heart tuned to what I was reading. I realized immediately, God is speaking to me through the words of this tiny book. I listened, I prayed the prayers before me, and I received complete and total deliverance from the oppression the enemy had drew me into. My dreams were fading, my health was failing, my emotions were raw and on my cuff.   In His time, He delivered me from eight months of turmoil, loss, sickness, and emotional trauma that was killing me. Today is a brighter day, because He gave birth in me, delivering me from the agony I was walking in. I am now, back on the narrow road, to birthing my Dreams, and walking in His footsteps. I recommend this book highly to the saved and unsaved, in need of a deliverance and renewal of the way, the truth, and the life.~**J.C. Beaver, Author**

Joyce Beaver

http://dreamingwithjc.weebly.com
http://facebook.com/joyce.beaver.9
http://joycebeaver6933.wordpress.com
http://twitter.com/jcb2blesJoyce

Table of Contents

INTRODUCTION

5 Steps to Birthing Your Dream A Spiritual Midwife's Manual

Do you need a midwife to help you give birth to your dreams?

Are you expecting your dreams to be fulfilled?

Are you the type of person, who, when your feet hit the floor, you're ready for the day to deliver something good to you? Or, are you the type of person that stumbles out of bed, wipes the sleep out of your eyes, and dreads your day?

I used to be the second type of person until I discovered my passion! Once I discovered what I "really, really" wanted, then my whole perspective changed and so did my expectation! I became big and pregnant, if you will, with a dream! This dream was in me all along. However, one day, as I was really feeling sorry for myself and thinking that my life really wasn't going anywhere, I decided to ask the Creator of the Universe, yes, God Himself, the Big Man upstairs, "Why?" Why was I created? What was my purpose? If you "really, really" want an answer, then brace yourself, because God will "really, really" give you an answer! However, I also must warn you! Once you find out the big "why".... prepare yourself to go on the most exciting journey of your life!

Why is this book necessary?

This book is necessary because women are broken and need help! This book will be a light in a dark place to many women who feel like it is too late for them to produce anything for the Kingdom. They feel like it is too late to birth their dreams, and truly be used of God. Many women are so broken, like I once was, to the point they can hardly imagine themselves ever being whole in order to birth anything for themselves, let, alone for others! This book is a step-by-step guide to take them from brokenness to breakthrough! If you can identify with some or all of what I just stated, than please read on as I am sure you will find answers and hope to dream again!

Maybe you feel as though you have your act altogether and you're highly successful and this book cannot possibly be for you. Perhaps not, but may I suggest you take a good hard look inside your heart, and make for sure.

Maybe after searching your heart, you still are great, I say wonderful, but how about other women in your life?
Would they benefit from this book? I dare say there is someone you may know who is broken. Maybe this book would be what she needs to be healed. Maybe she can experience the breakthrough she's longed for, or the kind of success you might be enjoying.

Since I've written this book with the dreamers in mind, from this point on, I am assuming I am talking to the kind of women that are as desperate as I was to birth their dreams. Are you ready for your new journey to begin?
Again, I can hear you saying, "I don't know if I'm ready or not!" You are, if you are asking all of the following questions.

Why do I want to birth a dream?

Your dreams are God given. God wants to use them to minister to others who need your talents and gifting. When your dreams are fulfilled, you will find they are the answer to someone else's question. God wants to fulfill your heart's desire, so you, yourself, will be fulfilled. He wants to prove His love to you so He can bless you extravagantly!

"What is God going to make me do? How do I know if it is God that's speaking to me? What if it is God speaking, then what? What if he tells me to do something, then how? What if I can't hear him speaking? What if, what if, what if???"

I'm here to help you get answers to all of those "what if" questions! But the first thing I want to address is fear! Fear is the opposite of faith. Fear is the number one weapon used by the enemy of your soul to hinder and delay all the wonderful dreams God has for you to birth! I want to assure you, the enemy has no power except what you allow him to have! So, like all women who have ever become pregnant, there is always a sense of anxiousness, because of the unknown element. However, when we focus on the wonderful miraculous process we walk through, then fear truly has no place. We can take each day and enjoy our journey!

Consider me to be like a Midwife! Once you've become pregnant with purpose, I am here to also help you give birth to your dream! I will walk you through the process, helping you with the following five steps! I will be here for you just like a midwife would be!

This book is a step-by-step guide to take many women from brokenness or barrenness to breakthrough!

5 Steps to Birthing Your Dream!

1.) Conceive:

I'll help you get yourself ready to receive and conceive what God has for you!

2.) Contend:
I'll help you fight or contend for the prize when you may feel like giving up! You will fulfill your purpose.

3.) Carry:
I'll be here to help you carry your promise and nourish it with the right stuff! You will carry your dream full term!

4.) Compel:
I'll compel you to push until you deliver your wonderful bouncing Dream!

5.) Complete:
I'll be here until your delivery is completed. You're created and purposed to give birth to your dreams!

Philippians1:6 Being confident of this very thing, that He which hath begun a good work in you will perform it until the day of Jesus Christ:

Are you ready? Let me warn you first, with a big red Warning! As with all births, it is not pretty! Birthing, although it is the most natural and beautiful thing God gave women to do, is not a pretty little job! No Mam, it is a dirty, messy job! It means you will pull strength out of a place that you never even imagined you had. It means you will sweat and wrestle within and without to get relieved of the thing you thought was such a gift just hours before labor! It is a process where there is no turning back, baby! You will give birth to that "**Holy thing**!" However, once you have delivered, Oh my, how your whole entire world is rocked forever!

So I ask again, "Are you ready?" If your answer is yes, then you must know in the natural, there are things you have to prepare in order to conceive. I am here to tell you, in the spiritual realm, there are things you must prepare for as well, in order to conceive spiritually.

I am here to encourage you. Come on my sister and my friend! We've got this, we are Women; but first, you must conceive.

Chapter One
Conceive

Jeremiah 29:11 For I know the thoughts that I think toward you, saith the Lord, thoughts of peace, and not of evil, to give you an expected end.

First and foremost, you are a Daughter of the Most High God! So why do you act as though you have no hope? Girl, you were born for such a time as this. You were born to conceive, and to carry a promise just like Mary, the mother of Jesus did. Why? So that what you birth will help build the Kingdom of God! I hear you say, "But that was Mary, I am just me!" I ask you, what is the difference between you and Mary? The only thing I see is obedience! When the angel appeared to Mary, and gave her the word of the Lord, she had a choice to believe or not to believe what she was hearing! Nothing began to happen to her until she had faith in the word she was hearing. You, too, have a choice to make. You can either choose to believe, or not to believe, as you read this that God has sent me to speak to you! Am I an angel? No, I am not an angel. However, I am sure I have a message for you, which is what angels usually do—they deliver messages. Like Mary, you can choose to believe what I am saying to you is true, or you can choose not to believe. It's up to you! My sincere hope is, you will believe. Once again, like Mary, you are chosen to receive from Heaven what God wants to birth through you on earth!

Let me show you, through scripture, that God used women mightily to birth in the Kingdom of God on earth! He still wants to continue to use women, just like you, to continue to give birth to the things of God! More than likely you've already been carrying the seed of it. You know, it is the thing you always go back to or desire to do. However, for whatever reason, you have been disappointed or discouraged, so you try to move on to something else. May I just say that your greatest joy will be when you realize that you, yes...You, are called to bear much fruit. God has great need of you my dear friend!

Luke 1: 5 There was in the days of Herod, the king of Judaea, a certain priest named Zacharias, of the course of Abia: and his wife was of the daughters of Aaron, and her name was Elisabeth.

6 And they were both righteous before God, walking in all the commandments and ordinances of the Lord blameless.

7 And they had no child, because that Elisabeth was barren, and they both were now well stricken in years.

8 And it came to pass, that while he executed the priest's office before God in the order of his course,

9 According to the custom of the priest's office, his lot was to burn incense when he went into the temple of the Lord.

10 And the whole multitude of the people were praying without at the time of incense.

11 And there appeared unto him an angel of the Lord standing on the right side of the altar of incense.

12 And when Zacharias saw him, he was troubled, and fear fell upon him.

13 But the angel said unto him, Fear not, Zacharias: for thy prayer is heard; and thy wife Elisabeth shall bear thee a son, and thou shalt call his name John.

14 And thou shalt have joy and gladness; and many shall rejoice at his birth.

15 For he shall be great in the sight of the Lord, and shall drink neither wine nor strong drink; and he shall be filled with the Holy Ghost, even from his mother's womb.

16 And many of the children of Israel shall he turn to the Lord their God.

17 And he shall go before him in the spirit and power of Elias, to turn the hearts of the fathers to the children, and the disobedient to the wisdom of the just; to make ready a people prepared for the Lord.

18 And Zacharias said unto the angel, Whereby shall I know this? for I am an old man, and my wife well stricken in years.

19 And the angel answering said unto him, I am Gabriel that stand in the presence of God; and am sent to speak unto thee, and to shew thee these glad tidings.
20 And, behold, thou shalt be dumb, and not able to speak, until the day that these things shall be performed, because thou believest not my words, which shall be fulfilled in their season.

21 And the people waited for Zacharias, and marveled that he tarried so long in the temple.

22 And when he came out, he could not speak unto them: and they perceived that he had seen a vision in the temple: for he beckoned unto them, and remained speechless.

23 And it came to pass, that, as soon as the days of his ministration were accomplished, he departed to his own house.

24 And after those days his wife Elisabeth conceived, and hid herself five months, saying,

25 Thus hath the Lord dealt with me in the days wherein he looked on me, to take away my reproach among men.

God did not call any of us to be barren or unfruitful. Maybe, like Elisabeth, you've been barren, and thought you could not conceive, but God can and will make a way where there seems to be no way! Maybe you've not been barren where children are concerned, but in other things, you've been barren. You've been brokenhearted. He will take away your reproach (disappointment or disapproval).

God is not withholding from you. He wants to position you for greatness so what you birth will be for a great purpose! He wants you to give birth to your dreams! You know those things that feel like they are simply too big, or just enough out of reach, you can't bring them forth!

I honestly can tell you, I know what it's like to desire something so badly, but remain barren. I know what it is like to be broken and hide it so well that if anyone actually knew, they would be surprised. I've lived through that experience for many years, but God gave me my heart's desire. He walked me through the desert place into a land of breakthrough and fruitfulness.

My husband and I were married for twenty years and could not conceive natural children. There wasn't anything physically wrong with either of us to prevent us from having a child. We even had a word from the Lord that we would have children. I believed that word with all my heart, but still I remained childless for many years. However, God's word is true and He is faithful to perform His great promises. His plans and ways do not always work on our schedule. Nor do they work the way we desire them to. He allowed me to become pregnant, and have the children I believed for in His time. They were born in this time and for this generation. Why? Because God knew my children would have more of an influence, and can reach more souls! They were born in a time where their voices need to be heard!

Elisabeth, in the New Testament, had a child who was born for a divine reason. Her child was, of course, John the Baptist, who was a forerunner of Jesus. Wow! What if Elisabeth would have said, "I don't believe God wants me to have my heart's desire." No, I'm not going to believe that I am to do this. I'm not going to try to have a baby in my old age. I just will not believe God wants me to have children. People will laugh at me and scorn me!" Thank God, Elisabeth didn't believe all the lies, but instead trusted the Lord to fulfill her heart's desire of having children.

Ladies, let me just tell you, there will always be those who will mock, who will make fun. The way to shut the mouths of the lions is to obey God, and let Him shut them up! You are "Highly favored!" The Lord wants you to conceive what He has to impart to you, so that you will birth that "**Holy thing**" upon the earth! Will you let what others think decide your future? I hope not!

Now, picture if you can, Elisabeth, big and pregnant, in her sixth month when the following occurred:

Luke1:26 And in the sixth month the angel Gabriel was sent from God unto a city of Galilee, named Nazareth,

27 To a virgin espoused to a man whose name was Joseph, of the house of David; and the virgin's name was Mary.
28 And the angel came in unto her, and said, Hail, thou that art highly favoured, the Lord is with thee: blessed art thou among women.

29 And when she saw him, she was troubled at his saying, and cast in her mind what manner of salutation this should be.

30 And the angel said unto her, Fear not, Mary: for thou hast found favour with God.

31 And, behold, thou shalt conceive in thy womb, and bring forth a son, and shalt call his name Jesus.

32 He shall be great, and shall be called the Son of the Highest: and the Lord God shall give unto him the throne of his father David:

33 And he shall reign over the house of Jacob forever; and of his kingdom there shall be no end.

34 Then said Mary unto the angel, How shall this be, seeing I know not a man?

35 And the angel answered and said unto her, The Holy Ghost shall come upon thee, and the power of the Highest shall overshadow thee: therefore also that Holy thing which shall be born of thee shall be called the Son of God.

36 And, behold, thy cousin Elisabeth, she hath also conceived a son in her old age: and this is the sixth month with her, who was called barren.

37 For with God nothing shall be impossible.

38 And Mary said, Behold the handmaid of the Lord; be it unto me according to thy word. And the angel departed from her.

39 And Mary arose in those days, and went into the hill country with haste, into a city of Juda;

40 And entered into the house of Zacharias, and saluted Elisabeth.

41 And it came to pass, that, when Elisabeth heard the salutation of Mary, the babe leaped in her womb; and Elisabeth was filled with the Holy Ghost:

42 And she spake out with a loud voice, and said, Blessed art thou among women, and blessed is the fruit of thy womb.

43 And whence is this to me that the mother of my Lord should come to me?

44 For, lo, as soon as the voice of thy salutation sounded in mine ears, the babe leaped in my womb for joy.
45 And blessed is she that believed: for there shall be a performance of those things which were told her from the Lord.

46 And Mary said, My soul doth magnify the Lord,

47 And my spirit hath rejoiced in God my Saviour.

48 For he hath regarded the low estate of his handmaiden: for, behold, from henceforth all generations shall call me blessed.

49 For he that is mighty hath done to me great things; and holy is his name.

50 And his mercy is on them that fear him from generation to generation.

51 He hath shewed strength with his arm; he hath scattered the proud in the imagination of their hearts.

52 He hath put down the mighty from their seats, and exalted them of low degree.

53 He hath filled the hungry with good things; and the rich he hath sent empty away.

54 He hath helped his servant Israel, in remembrance of his mercy;

55 As he spake to our fathers, to Abraham, and to his seed forever.

56 And Mary abode with her about three months, and returned to her own house.

57 Now Elisabeth's full time came that she should be delivered; and she brought forth a son.

58 And her neighbours and her cousins heard how the Lord had shewed great mercy upon her; and they rejoiced with her.

59 And it came to pass, that on the eighth day they came to circumcise the child; and they called him Zacharias, after the name of his father.

60 And his mother answered and said, Not so; but he shall be called John.

61 And they said unto her, There is none of thy kindred that is called by this name.

62 And they made signs to his father, how he would have him called.

63 And he asked for a writing table, and wrote, saying, His name is John. And they marvelled all.

64 And his mouth was opened immediately, and his tongue loosed, and he spake, and praised God.
65 And fear came on all that dwelt round about them: and all these sayings were noised abroad throughout all the hill country of Judaea.

66 And all they that heard them laid them up in their hearts, saying, What manner of child shall this be! And the hand of the Lord was with him.

67 And his father Zacharias was filled with the Holy Ghost, and prophesied, saying,

68 Blessed be the Lord God of Israel; for he hath visited and redeemed his people,

69 And hath raised up an horn of salvation for us in the house of his servant David;

70 As he spake by the mouth of his holy prophets, which have been since the world began:

71 That we should be saved from our enemies, and from the hand of all that hate us;

72 To perform the mercy promised to our fathers, and to remember his holy covenant;

73 The oath which he sware to our father Abraham,

74 That he would grant unto us, that we being delivered out of the hand of our enemies might serve him without fear,
75 In holiness and righteousness before him, all the days of our life.

76 And thou, child, shalt be called the prophet of the Highest: for thou shalt go before the face of the Lord to prepare his ways;

77 To give knowledge of salvation unto his people by the remission of their sins,

78 Through the tender mercy of our God; whereby the dayspring from on high hath visited us,

79 To give light to them that sit in darkness and in the shadow of death, to guide our feet into the way of peace.

80 And the child grew, and waxed strong in spirit, and was in the deserts till the day of his shewing unto Israel.

Again, you may be saying, "But that was Mary!" But, I will say to you without trying to offend anyone, Mary was just an ordinary girl who found the favor of the Lord. She, like Elisabeth, had a choice to accept what God had planned for her or not! She chose to trust and believe the Word of the Lord. So, I ask you, are you going to trust that you are hearing the Word of the Lord at this very moment? If so, you can say, like Mary, "Behold the handmaid of the Lord; be it unto me according to thy Word." Do you realize that the word of the Lord is the seed?

When you receive the word of the Lord as truth and act upon it, the seed of His Word causes you to conceive and believe all things are possible. As that seed continues to grow, you will give birth to what it has produced, which is your dreams and God's purpose for your life!

Will you please pray this prayer with me? We are going to believe for conception to take place and that you will conceive what God wants you to birth in Jesus name!

Dear Lord, I receive your words of promise that I am created to birth "**Holy things**" for the Kingdom of God. I will say with Mary, "Behold the handmaid of the Lord; be it unto me according to thy Word." Thank you that as I believe your words of promise which are Yes and Amen, I am conceiving what you sent it to produce in me In Jesus name. I am pregnant with the promise of the Word of the Lord in Jesus' name. I thank you that my dreams will no longer be delayed or deferred, but will be a tree of life so that others can come and partake!

Proverbs 13:12 Hope deferred makes a heart sick, but when the desires comes it is a tree of life.

Chapter Two

Contend!

Now that you have finally conceived, what do you do? You must contend or you must do a good warfare, like a soldier, in order to carry your dream full term! Yes, you might be saying as you read this, "This lady is nuts! What does she think I've been doing all of this time?" First, let me assure you, please do not fear, the battle is not yours, it belongs to the Lord. However, you must set your face like a flint so as not to be moved! I call you soldier, because you have already been in the trenches interceding for your Dream and have prevailed! You're triumphant in battle! The victory is that you've conceived your Dream or Dreams! You are a Mighty Woman of Faith! You can do this thing of birthing God given Dreams that will bring His Kingdom to those that need your gifts and talents! Once your Dream is birthed, it will be like a stone skipped on top of the water! It will cause a rippling effect and touch many lives! So what do you have to do?

James 4:7 Submit yourselves therefore to God. Resist the devil, and he will flee from you.

I know this seems simple enough, but the enemy doesn't play fair at all. He is a schemer, who uses lies and deceit to try to convince his victims of his lies. Again, I said all of this, only to prepare you! The enemy has held you back all of this time, and he does not like to lose, but he is already defeated. When he was thrown out of the garden, the Lord spoke to him, telling him, the heel of the seed of the woman would bruise his head!

Genesis 3:15 And I will put enmity between thee and the woman, and between thy seed and her seed; it shall bruise thy head, and thou shalt bruise his heel.

Again, women have always played such an important role in the Kingdom of God. As we know by scripture, Jesus was born of a woman and defeated Satan once and for all! All we have to do is stand in what Jesus did for us on the cross, submit ourselves to God and resist the devil! We must also realize that what Jesus did on the cross is enough.

You may be reading this and saying, "But I am not a Christian and I do not believe all of that!"

My answer to you is, 'why not?' Although I am writing to Christian women, I don't think you are reading this by accident, especially if you've gotten this far. You are obviously hungry for something. So, I must ask again, why aren't you a Christian? Why wouldn't you believe in a wonderful God who loved you so much, He gave His most precious gift to win your heart! He looked ahead in time, while you weren't even conceived yet! He planned out your life to be here right now to hear that He has created you to shower His love upon you. He wants you to be blessed and great! You may be saying, "Well my life has been horrible! Where has this wonderful God been all of this time?"

Again, my answer to you is, 'He is right where He has always been!' He is at the door, knocking on your heart, wanting to be let in. However, He is a true gentleman and will not force himself on anyone. He has to be invited in, which I truly hope you will do right now!

Please pray this prayer with me!

"Lord Jesus, come into my heart and make all things new! I turn from all other gods and ask that you forgive me of all my sins. I believe that you, Jesus, died for my sins. I believe that you rose again on the third day so that I can have a brand new life! I want to serve you with all of my heart. Use me to birth what you have already placed in my heart to birth! Thank you that I am born again and that my life is brand new in Jesus name!"

Now if you asked him to come into your heart and make all things new, I have wonderful news… He did! Yes, it is that simple. He loves you and delights to come in. Starting this very moment, you are born again and your spirit has been made brand new!

My reference for contending again is simply natural pregnancy and the word of God! I believe the Lord gave us the natural to help us understand and truly be able to relate to the spiritual. I love the parables of Jesus and draw reference to them to help you. Jesus used practical teaching about farming, planting, fig trees, and red skies, precious coins, talents and other relatable things, and yes, even labor pains etc., to help those he taught. He used simple things to help them understand the spiritual principles he was trying to convey to them. I want to do much the same thing to help you.

If you are anything like I was, you are euphoric about conceiving and cannot thank or Praise God enough! You take a deep breath and reflect back at how you stood fast in the presence of God, and Satan, to believe for conception of this dream that you are ready to birth! The thoughts of it are real one minute and then seem like an Illusion the next! Perhaps in the natural, you've taken the physical pregnancy test and you've gotten proof! Or, God's confirmed it to you spiritually over and over again. When the enemy comes, and he will come immediately to try to steal the word that has been planted into your heart, just know God's Word has been conceived in your heart (spiritual womb)! No more illusion here, even though your soul, which is your mind, will, emotions and intellect scream out, "Can this really be?" Let peace come from your spirit assuring you, "Yes, indeed this can be and is!"

When you are physically pregnant, you can't wait to call all of your family and friends so they will celebrate with you! Joy overwhelms you and you find yourself a hormonal mess crying and blowing your nose into boxes of tissues! Can I just be real for a moment? Not to be a party pooper or anything to stop your celebration, because the Lord wants you to be excited and filled with joy, but when you are physically pregnant, it is easy for your family to rejoice with you as they can see evidence of a pregnancy being there; but unfortunately, when you are pregnant with a spiritual pregnancy or dream, you may not get the same enthusiasm. I truly hope that you will, however, it has been my experience that unless people, including those wonderful people who are the closest to us, can see or have proof of a baby, they will have trouble rejoicing with you.

As a spiritual midwife, I rejoice with you and have no greater joy than to help you bring this "**Holy thing**" into the world! However, as with any natural midwife, I feel I must prepare you and let you know what to expect physically and spiritually.

For example: During my physical pregnancies, it was like getting on a rollercoaster ride. I only thought I was on a rollercoaster ride while trying to conceive because, again, it took my husband and I twenty years; but Honey, I never knew what a rollercoaster ride was, until I actually did conceive! I was elated one moment and terrified the next.

I was elated when I thought of holding that precious long awaited bundle in my arms, but terrified of the actual birthing process! As I found myself vomiting every morning, noon, and evening with "morning sickness," I became even more fearful that I was not cut out to do this! The enemy's onslaught of spiritual accusations and the physical changes in my body never let up! When I would think about that same little precious thing relying on me to take good care of it, every doubt about my inabilities to take care of a baby overwhelmed me. What did I know about nurturing a baby, or this Dream that God wanted me to birth? How do I raise this child in the fear and admonition of the Lord? Or, how can I use this Dream to give honor unto the Lord? My hormones raged and so did the enemy! All I could hear was, "What if I can't do this? What if I can't do that? What if I do something horrible and scar the baby for life? What if....what if?" But suddenly, when it seemed as though the enemy was winning his battle, I had a "light bulb moment" if you will, a Rhema word from the Lord. If God, the very God of the Universe, the God of all that was and will ever be, gave me this precious dream, **"Holy thing"** to be birthed, then He fully intended on helping me! He was co-laboring with me to nurture it, and take good care of it! Just as it took the word to conceive this **"Holy thing,"** it was still going to take His Word to carry the Dream full term!

During my pregnancy and the battle that raged in my emotions, the Lord spoke to me and told me to "Tell the

Enemy to Scat!" Now, you may not know the reference to that word and may find it hard to relate to, but being a little farm girl from Kentucky, I knew exactly what that word meant. This is what we would say to our barn cats that tried to get into the house. We would physically stomp our feet on the porch to scare them away and tell them to "Scat!" Where does the Lord say that the enemy should be? Didn't He say that the enemy should be under our feet?" Well, once He gave me my word, let me tell you, I began stomping, and I would speak out loud to the enemy and tell him to "Scat!" Do you know what happened? Yes, indeed, the enemy left me! Finally, my long awaited pregnancy was a joy until I gave birth!

As you read this midwife's manual, I hope that the words will be your Rhema word, which is a word that comes alive in your spirit to help you go forward. I want to declare that you are armed with the Life of God and His Word! I hope this manual will encourage you to arise, stand strong on your feet, walk into a place that the enemy has kept you defeated and down, and speak boldly to the enemy of your soul!

"Devil, I've put up with your stuff long enough! You are the father of all lies, and I refuse to believe them over myself any longer!" Now stomp, and command him to "Scat!"

Chapter Three

Carry

So you've conceived your dream! You've been contending for it. Now it's time to carry your dream full term! We do not want any miscarriages or aborted dreams!

Now on with the carrying of your dream! When a woman is expecting a baby, she will go through a nesting phase, especially when she begins to feel little movements or maybe begins to show a little. This is a phase where she wants to create a safe and happy, nurturing place for her baby to come home to. She usually empties out a room that she has stored a bunch of "stuff" in. She throws out a bunch of the "stuff" that was once important, but now doesn't seem worth holding on to. Of course, she does this in the natural, but may I suggest that you do the same thing spiritually.

Where are you going to nurture your dreams? Do you have a safe place you can bring them home to? Do you have to clear out a bunch of "stuff" to make room for them? Most of us come from areas of brokenness in our lives. Maybe you never did. If you didn't, that is simply wonderful, but if you did, then you know what "stuff" you probably need to throw out. When a woman is pregnant in the natural, she already carries extra "weight"; so to carry excess "stuff" would simply be too stressful for her. So it will be for you as well. You may be asking, "How do I get rid of the 'stuff'?"

At first let me point out some "stuff." Maybe it was abuse. Maybe you were emotionally and/or physically abused as a child or as an adult. Maybe you've been hurt by people you trusted. Maybe you were hurt by a Pastor, or church member. Maybe you were abandoned, or rejected, or bullied etc. Now you are getting the idea and probably can immediately name someone or several people who have hurt you. Don't you think you've let that "stuff" rob and steal enough from you? Do you want to get rid of it? If so, continue reading please.

Below is the number one prayer I believe will get rid of a lot of the "stuff" in your life. If you sincerely pray this prayer and mean it with all of your heart, I believe it will truly give you the power to walk out your dreams you've longed to walk in and do, for years. Yes, I know this is a bold statement, but may I share with you what I've experienced in twenty years of ministry to be the number one thing keeping a person bound up in "stuff" and fear?

It is unforgiveness. Yes, I hear you, again, saying, "But you don't know how badly that person has hurt me." No, I might not be able to perceive your pain and heartaches, but this thing I know, the person who offended you or hurt you has more than likely went on to live a full and productive life. They've never once looked back, or gave you a second thought. I know that sounds harsh, but I say that to say this, 'You've stopped living or moving forward,' because you are tied to that past event and person. It's like they are tied to your back. The weight of carrying them is one reason, if not the main reason, you feel stuck and can't go forward. It's caused you to miscarry many of your dreams or abort them, altogether.

Would you please pray with me? This is not a prayer that you may feel like praying, but do you know faith isn't about how you feel? It is about what you believe. If you believe what I just told you is the truth about being weighted down, then I want you to trust our God has brought you to this very crucial and divine point to meet with you. He wants to deliver you from the weight of all your burdens. If you want to be free from the weight of carrying unforgiveness, then please pray this prayer with me!

Dear Heavenly Father,

I have been consumed by the hurt and pain of what (put in the name or names of the people) _____ did to me all of these years. I do not want this pain to hinder me any longer. I give it to you. I, by an act of my will, not necessarily my emotions, release _____ from everything they've done to hurt me. There is nothing they can do to pay back the debt they owe me, but Lord you took all of it, theirs and mine, so I lay everything down. As I release them, Lord, I ask you to cleanse me from the heartache and the bitterness. Lord, cause this open wound to be healed over. Lord, I may always carry the scar to remind me, but I do not ever want to carry the pain any longer. Thank you Father, you meet me right where I am. All those things in my life that the enemy has used to break me are now my testimonies of Breakthrough. These are the very things you will use to promote me, so I can be used to help others, who were just like me, to gain freedom! Thank you Lord, I am free in Jesus name!

James 4:7 Submit yourselves therefore to God. Resist the devil, and he will flee from you.

You might be saying to yourself, "Now, really, it doesn't take all that. It is normal to go through mixed emotions and wonder if you can go through pregnancy and then labor."

I mean no disrespect at all, if you are a woman reading this, and this is your stance, but maybe, you are not the one I am actually speaking to! I am speaking to the Desperate Dreamers! The Dreamers I am speaking to are the women who have longed for years to see their dreams come to pass and it seems every door they knocked on is slammed in their faces. I am speaking to those who have cried themselves to sleep, night after night, because the life they now live looks nothing like the life they envisioned, neither does it feel like the life the Lord promised them they could have. I am speaking to those women who feel like they are barren and ashamed because they seemingly have nothing to offer. I am speaking to those women who have gone through painful miscarriages, both physically and spiritually, which left them feeling empty and alone! I am speaking to those women who have been so tormented by the accuser; they find it difficult to ever imagine their lives could be fruitful. I am speaking to those women who think it is an even crazier idea that they could be used to minister life to others who have gone through what they've experienced or are currently going through it! No, if you do not fit in one of these categories, I am not speaking to you!

Am I saying that carrying a Dream is all woes, struggles, and sickness, and that you should be scared to try to birth it? Absolutely not, but what I am trying to convey is: NOW that the Lord has birthed that **"Holy thing"** in you, you have a very real adversary who will come immediately and try to steal it!

Mark 4 (KJV) And he began again to teach by the sea side: and there was gathered unto him a great multitude, so that he entered into a ship, and sat in the sea; and the whole multitude was by the sea on the land.

2 And he taught them many things by parables, and said unto them in his doctrine,
3 Hearken; Behold, there went out a sower to sow:
4 And it came to pass, as he sowed, some fell by the way side, and the fowls of the air came and devoured it up.

5 And some fell on stony ground, where it had not much earth; and immediately it sprang up, because it had no depth of earth:

6 But when the sun was up, it was scorched; and because it had no root, it withered away.

7 And some fell among thorns, and the thorns grew up, and choked it, and it yielded no fruit.

8 And other fell on good ground, and did yield fruit that sprang up and increased; and brought forth, some thirty, and some sixty, and some an hundred.

9 And he said unto them, He that hath ears to hear, let him hear.
10 And when he was alone, they that were about him with the twelve asked of him the parable.

11 And he said unto them, Unto you it is given to know the mystery of the kingdom of God: but unto them that are without, all these things are done in parables:

12 That seeing they may see, and not perceive; and hearing they may hear, and not understand; lest at any time they should be converted, and their sins should be forgiven them.

13 And he said unto them, Know ye not this parable? and how then will ye know all parables?

14 The sower soweth the word.

15 And these are they by the way side, where the word is sown; but when they have heard, Satan cometh immediately, and taketh away the word that was sown in their hearts.

16 And these are they likewise which are sown on stony ground; who, when they have heard the word, immediately receive it with gladness;

17 And have no root in themselves, and so endure but for a time: afterward, when affliction or persecution ariseth for the word's sake, immediately they are offended.

18 And these are they which are sown among thorns; such as hear the word,

19 And the cares of this world, and the deceitfulness of riches, and the lusts of other things entering in, choke the word, and it becometh unfruitful.

20 And these are they which are sown on good ground; such as hear the word, and receive it, and bring forth fruit, some thirtyfold, some sixty, and some an hundred.

21 And he said unto them, Is a candle brought to be put under a bushel, or under a bed? and not to be set on a candlestick?

22 For there is nothing hid, which shall not be manifested; neither was anything kept secret, but that it should come abroad.

23 If any man have ears to hear, let him hear.

I am not talking to women who do not know this! You could probably write a better book than I, on what all has been stolen; however, the enemy has silenced you by his onslaught of torment to keep you from trying again. This is why I am writing to you! I want the words of this book to break off the lies of the enemy which keep you in a place of always wishing for better, but never really seeing it. I hope to encourage you to see the enemy may have won a few victories, but you are still here! You are still breathing! Honestly deep down, even while you are afraid, you are still hoping the Lord will help you bring forth your lifelong dreams! I am here to help you like a good midwife does. I want to encourage you by convincing you that you are an overcomer and even more than an overcomer, according to the Word of God! Yes, you might have gone through hell, without understanding why you had to go through it, but the point is: God's promises to you are still Yes and Amen! You are still standing, girlfriend!

I wish only to prepare you, so that you can equip yourself, or arm yourself with the Word of God. You can defeat your enemy every time you act in faith! This is how you carry your Dream! You must build yourself upon your most holy faith! Be confident all of you who are pregnant with that "**Holy thing**." You always, always have God on your side! I have included some wonderful scripture that helped me to conceive, contend and carry, what God has put in me to birth into the Kingdom. What I am sharing with you is a manual full of scripture that is full proof, when mixed with faith, to cause you to not only birth the "**Holy thing**" you are expecting now, but will continue to help you birth all the spiritual babies or "**Holy things**" God has planned for you to birth in the future. Grab a hold of this scripture, take it like medicine when the enemy comes physically to challenge you, take it up like a sword when he launches an assault against you spiritually, hold on to it like a life preserver when the waves seem to overwhelm you, for the Word of God is a sure foundation that cannot be shaken. Jesus is the rock that cannot be moved, so be encouraged, Dear Sister, Fellow Woman of God, Mighty Woman of Faith, and Highly Favored of the Lord. You've got this because God's got you!

Romans 8:31 What shall we then say to these things? If God be for us, who can be against us?

32 He that spared not his own Son, but delivered him up for us all, how shall he not with him also freely give us all things?

33 Who shall lay anything to the charge of God's elect? It is God that justifieth.

34 Who is he that condemneth? It is Christ that died, yea rather, that is risen again, who is even at the right hand of God, who also maketh intercession for us.

Chapter 4
Compel

While the "**Holy thing**" you are carrying is growing larger and larger, the evidence of things hoped for are truly showing! As your dreams are growing, there will be times, as the day of delivery draws closer, when you may become very uncomfortable in every area of your being—spirit, soul, and body. The enemy of your soul (mind, will, emotions, and intellect) is the accuser and unfortunately, he does his job very well. He will always try to use self-doubt, lies, and your past, to try to prevent you from birthing the "**Holy thing**" which will change not only your future, but the futures of many you will minister to. Do not believe his lies or fear him, for the God of all peace and comfort wants to assure you that you were created for such a time as this.

When we walk through places of unfamiliarity, it is natural to be a little unsure of ourselves. However, we can be peaceful, because, if God has led you to it, He will surely lead you through it! I think of the Israelites in the wilderness. Their trip lasted for forty years because they kept looking back to Egypt. Egypt was a place of horrible oppression for them, but it was familiar. What the Israelites had to look forward to, was a wonderful promise land. This was a land flowing full of milk and honey. The promise land was full of their hopes and dreams, but they let the fear of giants and the way they saw themselves cheat them out of what God had for them. I compel you, please do not look back, you are at the threshold of open doors to walk through to obtain your dreams. Do not let the enemy convince you this "**Holy thing**" was never for you! See yourself as God sees you! If you will, then nothing can stop you!

As a midwife, I am here to compel you or to urge you to push your way through the unfamiliar process! The Bible story of the woman with the issue of blood is brought to mind when I think of how a woman has to push to have a baby. You may remember the Bible story of the woman who had the issue where she was afflicted with pain and bleeding for eighteen long years. She had a very difficult choice to make one day, as she heard about Jesus healing people. Would she stay in the place of debilitating pain and let her issues control her another eighteen years? Or, would she press and push her way through to touch Jesus? You must realize how desperate this woman had become. To come out into the public, she risked being stoned, because she was considered to be unclean. The story, of course, ends well as she was able to touch the very hem of Jesus' garment which represented the Word of God. She was healed and made completely whole; but do you know what was striking to me about that story? Even after she was healed, she tried to remain hidden and bent over. However, Jesus didn't want her to ever feel rejected again. He went and lifted her up himself for all to see that she was there. He let her know she was valuable. We've all had issues at one time or the other that hindered us, or delayed us, or, in some cases, totally stole from us what we were supposed to have accomplished. But like the woman who had the issue in the Bible, I am compelling you to press! Push your way to Jesus! Be made completely whole and well.

You've gone through a lot to get to this point. You are in the end of your final trimester. Everything about your body has changed in preparation for birth, but something else has had to change as well. You had to change your mindsets on a number of things as you went through this process of birthing your dreams! Mindsets are so important to birthing your dreams! Rise up my Sister; walk up right, with your head held high, for the Lord Himself has come to lift you out of your issues as well! He wants you to continue to walk in the freedom He has provided for you, not only to walk out this Dream, but all of the others that you will birth for His Kingdom.

Now comes the time you have been waiting for. However, this is the most crucial and important part yet—the labor.

This is the time when you make everything you believed God for, count. This is the time to birth that "**Holy thing**"! This is the time where there is no turning back like the Israelites, or like the woman with the issue who pressed in! This is the time where all you stood for, all you conceived, contended, carried and were compelled to birth is coming to pass! This is the time the contractions have started, and the long job of laboring has begun. Suddenly, something gushes out that up until this point had kept your dreams or baby in a protective place. Now the true travailing is eminent!

John 16:20 (KJV) Verily, verily, I say unto you, that ye shall weep and lament, but the world shall rejoice: and ye shall be sorrowful, but your sorrow shall be turned into joy.

21 A woman when she is in travail hath sorrow, because her hour is come: but as soon as she is delivered of the child, she remembereth no more the anguish, for joy that a man is born into the world.

There are several stages of labor and with each one; the labor pains become more and more intense as the contractions become closer and closer together. It is the midwife's job to help you to keep focused on the joy of the end result. With each breathtaking pain, the "Holy thing" becomes more and more real. Finally, you are as desperate to rid yourself of the "Holy thing," as you were desperate to conceive it! When you are desperate for relief, you will push. I've heard many Christians over the years give a definition of what they thought the word

Push meant: "Push, Until Something Happens!" I do not know who came up with that, but honestly, you are on the verge of one of the greatest things in the world ever happening to you. I want to coach you and compel you to PUSH! "Push, Until Something Happens!" Push, as the pains come closer and harder! Push, because you have made it this far, Woman of God! Push, because with every push, your dreams become more real! The contractions are close enough now; you can physically touch and feel your dreams! Push, because you're right there on the edge! Push, Push, Push! I know you're exhausted, hot and sweaty. Push, even though you do not feel like you do have any more strength! Come on, just one more time, bare down and Push hard. Okay, this is the final time, Push....until your dream, your "**Holy thing**" cries out! Do you hear it? Can you see it? Can you touch it?

Chapter Five

Complete

Wow! You did well, Mighty Woman of God, who was created to birth this precious "Holy thing!" The thing you felt like would kill you, helped you to realize how very strong in God you are! You are complete in Him! Now what? Like every baby brought into the world or (Kingdom), it is time to nurture it, treasure it, guard it, and to protect it. You must take responsibility for what you have birthed. It was born for such a time as this. Now, it must be raised up! Again, I know it may seem like another daunting task, but just as you trusted God to conceive it, contend for it, carry it, and were compelled to deliver it, you must complete the purpose of the dream or reason for its birthing. The task is not yours alone! God will never leave you or forsake you. He fully intends to co-labor with you. Co-laboring with God will assure your dreams can reach their fullest potential. You came all of this long way. This was the very thing you were created to do. This "**Holy thing**!" has come to change nations and to bring the Kingdom of Heaven to earth! What probably is even more awesome is the change, and the impact it has had in you!

May I also say, as a Spiritual Midwife, I have great joy in helping you to see your dreams fulfilled?

My dreams, which are my sons, are now sixteen and twelve. I have truly enjoyed every day with them. I've treasured my time and sigh very heavily at the thoughts of the time when they will leave home. However, when I received my promises, they came with conditions. The Lord told me they would be prophets to the nations. Were these boys my only dreams? No! This book is a fulfillment of one of my dreams. It is just one of the "**Holy things**" the Lord wanted me to birth. Just as my sons were birthed to be used of God, so this book was birthed to be used by God to help you with birthing your dreams.

My heart's desire for this book is to change you, the reader, or perhaps for you to share it with someone you know who will benefit from its pages. May God bless you, and give you all of your heart's desires!

May All Your Dreams Come True!

About the Author

Christine Gilliam Hornback is a wife of thirty five years and a mother of two boys ages sixteen and twelve. She homeschools her children and is an Author, Artist, Art Instructor, and an Inspirational speaker. Christine has lived in Douglasville, Georgia for Thirty One years where she has been in Women's Ministry for over 20 of those years! She has encouraged and taught others through her writings, Inspirational speaking, and art, as she has had the opportunity to speak at annual ministry conferences, homeschool groups, local libraries, and community centers. She is an author of six published books. Christine is also a weekly blogger and is a regular contributor to Lakeview Times Online Magazine and Newspaper.

Contact Information:
Email:
chornback@bellsouth.net or
covenantessentials@gmail.com

Website:
http:// www.covenantessentials.com

Author Page:
https://www.amazon.com/Christine-
Hornback/e/B00J43R78C/ref=ntt_dp_epwbk_0

Facebook:
https://www.facebook.com/AuthorArtistMomOf2/

Twitter:
https://twitter.com/haveaheart4him

Blog:
http://authorartistmomof2.wordpress.com/

FREE BONUS GIFT
Tell the Enemy to Scat!

I wanted to take this time to thank you for purchasing my latest book by gifting you with a **Bonus Gift!** This ebook is the true testimony of my Dreams being fulfilled after 20 Long years! I reference this testimony in **5 Steps to Birthing Your Dream!** God is not finished, He wants to encourage you and help you to passionately fulfill your dreams! Simply follow the link to get your FREE copy of *Tell the Enemy to Scat!*

https://covenantessentials.leadpages.co/christines-encouragement/

Christine's Other Books!

All of Christine's books can be found easily on her
Amazon Author Page!
https://www.amazon.com/Christine-
Hornback/e/B00J43R78C/ref=dp_byline_cont_ebooks_1

Jenny Lynn's Secret Mission
Juvenile Fiction

Caleb's Cereal
Juvenile Fiction

If Oak Trees Could Talk
Romance/Suspense Novel

Mazy's High Flying Adventure
Juvenile Fiction

Mazy's High Flying Adventure!

2 Bonus Stories: Sable the Pony and Curley Sue's Lesson

Christine Gilliam Hornback

Made in the USA
Middletown, DE
25 February 2021

34421458R00035